EXTREME PLACES

The Tallest Building

Janet Halfmann

KIDHAVEN
PRESS™

THOMSON

GALE

San Diego • Detroit • New York • San Francisco • Cleveland
New Haven, Conn. • Waterville, Maine • London • Munich

© 2004 by KidHaven Press. KidHaven Press is an imprint of The Gale Group, Inc., a division of Thomson Learning, Inc.

KidHaven™ and Thomson Learning™ are trademarks used herein under license.

For more information, contact
KidHaven Press
27500 Drake Rd.
Farmington Hills, MI 48331-3535
Or you can visit our Internet site at http://www.gale.com

LIBRARY OF CONGRESS CATALOGING-IN-PUBLICATION DATA

Halfmann, Janet.
    The tallest building / by Janet Halfmann.
    p. cm. — (Extreme places)
Summary: Explains the purpose, design, construction, and costs of the Petronas Twin Towers in Kuala Lumpur, Malaysia.
Includes bibliographical references and index.
    ISBN 0-7377-1374-7 (hardback : alk. paper)
    1. Menara Berkembar Petronas (Kuala Lumpur, Malaysia)—Juvenile literature. 2. Office buildings—Malaysia—Kuala Lumpur—Juvenile literature. 3. Skyscrapers—Malaysia—Kuala Lumpur—Juvenile literature. 4. Kuala Lumpur (Malaysia)—Buildings, structures, etc.—Juvenile literature. [1. Petronas Twin Towers (Kuala Lumpur, Malaysia) 2. Skyscrapers.] I. Title. II. Series.
NA6234.M42K834 2004
720'.483'095951—dc21
                                                                2003009946

Printed in the United States of America

Contents

A Soaring Symbol

In the center of Kuala Lumpur, the busy, modern capital city of Malaysia, twin stainless steel skyscrapers soar skyward. Called the Petronas Twin Towers, they are the tallest buildings in Southeast Asia—and in the world. The spires, or **pinnacles**, of the slim, tapering towers rise 1,483 feet above the city.

Completed in 1996, the Petronas Twin Towers were built as a symbol of Malaysia's pride. The prime minister of this country of 23 million people summed up the symbolic importance of the towers at the festive grand opening. A nation that is small like Malaysia needs a sky-high boost to its pride, he explained. "When one is short, one should stand on a box to get a better view," he told the

The grand opening of the Petronas Twin Towers, the world's tallest buildings, is celebrated with colorful lights.

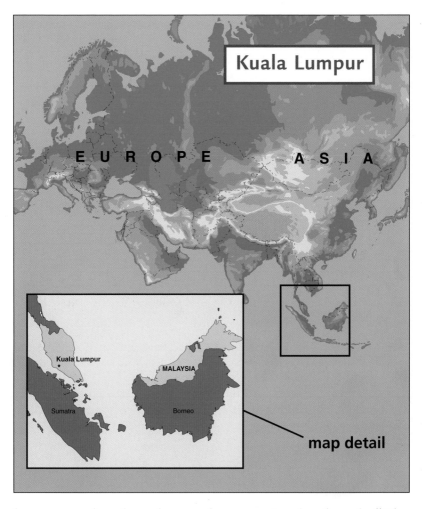

Kuala Lumpur

EUROPE   ASIA

Kuala Lumpur

MALAYSIA

Sumatra   Borneo

map detail

huge crowd gathered near the towering landmark. "The (Petronas) Twin Towers is to our ego what the box is to the shortie."[1]

The two eighty-eight-story towers, linked high in the air by a double-deck skybridge, contain space equal to ninety-six football fields with offices for thousands of workers. The towers are occupied by Petronas, the government-owned national oil company, and other large companies. The tower complex also features an 864-seat concert hall, an art gallery, a six-story shopping mall, a science center simulating life on an oil rig, and underground parking for five thousand cars. Each tower has a prayer room for observant Muslims, who pray five times a day.

The towers are the crowning jewel of a one-hundred-acre city-within-a-city started in 1992 at the heart of Kuala Lumpur's business district. The Petronas Twin Towers serve as a magnificent gateway to this development called the Kuala Lumpur City Center. The center includes a hotel, office towers, shops, restaurants, chilled-water plants to cool the buildings, and a gleaming marble **mosque** for six thousand worshipers. The buildings surround a fifty-acre playground and public park with jogging paths and two thousand trees.

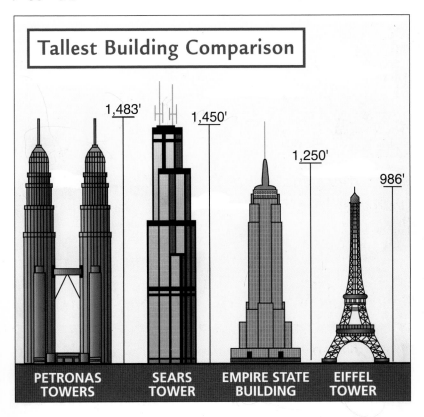

Tallest Building Comparison

1,483' | 1,450' | 1,250' | 986'

PETRONAS TOWERS | SEARS TOWER | EMPIRE STATE BUILDING | EIFFEL TOWER

Tallest of the Tall

The Petronas Twin Towers are two of only about twenty-five skyscrapers in the world to soar skyward more than 1,000 feet. By most accounts next tallest after the Petronas Twin Towers is the Sears Tower in Chicago, Illinois. It rises to 1,450 feet. This ranking of the world's tallest and next tallest buildings has been the subject of debate.

The Petronas Twin Towers did not start out to be the tallest buildings in the world. Architect Cesar Pelli describes the original plan in his book about the project. "That the towers should become the tallest buildings in the world was never discussed," he writes, "only that they be beautiful and could become new symbols of the growing importance of the Petronas Company and the city of Kuala Lumpur." [2]

These sketches by architect Cesar Pelli show the towers from an artistic point of view. They were designed to be beautiful.

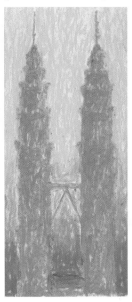  

This mosque near Kuala Lumpur has four minarets. The pinnacles of the Petronas Twin Towers are modeled after prayer towers like these.

Pelli's design called for two buildings that would rise 1,247 feet. Pointed tops would add to the look of the tall, slim buildings. But at some point in the project, Pelli decided he wanted a more tapered look. To get this look, the architects created six steps, like a staircase, in the upper part of the buildings. The upper walls also tilt slightly inward. These changes, Pelli says, made it necessary to rethink the very top of the towers. The pointed tops no longer looked right on the very tapered buildings. Something more was needed to project them into the heavens. After months of trial and error, the designers and owners agreed on slim stainless steel pinnacles modeled after Islamic **minarets,** or prayer towers, common in Malaysia.

Going for the Record

The addition of pinnacles greatly increased the height of the towers. Other changes, such as raising the floors to make room beneath them for computer cables and other wiring, added still more height. But the towers still were not the tallest in the world.

That achievement came about only after a casual conversation between Malaysia's prime minister and Pelli. The prime minister wondered how much taller the towers would have to be to capture the world height record. The answer was only about seventy-five feet. The buildings' owners decided to reach for the record. The designers did many calculations to determine if extra height could be added. They decided the best way to make the towers taller was by increasing the height of the pinnacles to an astounding 241 feet. The towers were on their way to winning the record.

When the Petronas Twin Towers were completed in 1996, they were named the tallest buildings in the world. This decision was made by the Council on Tall Buildings and Urban Habitat. This group is considered the international referee on height records for buildings around the world. Its members include architects, engineers, and other professionals who build tall buildings. The council based its decision on a sixty-year-old rule that says a building is to be measured from the sidewalk level of its main entrance to its structural top. Spires are to be included but not television and radio antennas or flagpoles. Under this rule the Petronas Twin Towers measure thirty-three feet taller than Chicago's Sears Tower.

The pinnacles of the towers add enough height to make them the world's tallest buildings (left). Cesar Pelli discusses a model of the pinnacles with his colleagues (right).

Chicago Fights Back

This decision caused an uproar in Chicago, which had boasted the tallest building for more than twenty years. The city did not want to give up the pride, prestige, and worldwide attention that comes with having the tallest building. Chicagoans fought to have the rule changed. They argued that height should be measured

11

The Sears Tower stands near Lake Michigan. Before the Petronas Twin Towers were built, the Chicago landmark was the tallest building in the world.

by a building's floors and not by its spires. The Sears Tower has 110 floors while the Petronas Twin Towers have 88. If buildings were measured from the main entrance to the highest occupied floor, the Sears Tower would be 1,431 feet, the Petronas Twin Towers would be 1,229 feet.

In an effort to keep peace in the world of tall buildings, the council compromised. It established four tallest building categories: height to the structural top; height to the highest occupied floor; height to the top of the roof; and height to the tip of the spire, pinnacle, antenna, mast, or flagpole. The Petronas Twin Towers retained the title in the first category. The Sears Tower holds the record in the other three categories. By tradition the first category remains the leading measure of the world's tallest building. As taller buildings take shape on the ground or on drawing boards around the world, the Petronas Twin Towers are considered the buildings to overtake in the race upward.

Designing Towers to Reach the Sky

S leek horses once raced around a track where the Petronas Twin Towers now stand. On race days traffic jams clogged the center of the city. So, in the 1980s, the government of Malaysia decided the racetrack should move to the edge of the city. With the move a huge chunk of land right in the heart of the city's business district became available for building. In 1990 the new owners of the land held an international competition to come up with a **master plan** for the entire one-hundred-acre site. The plan that was selected mapped out the Kuala Lumpur City Center. The highlight of the plan was two tall, showcase towers to house a new world headquarters for the wealthy Petronas oil company. Eight architectural firms experienced in designing tall buildings were invited to submit designs for the show-

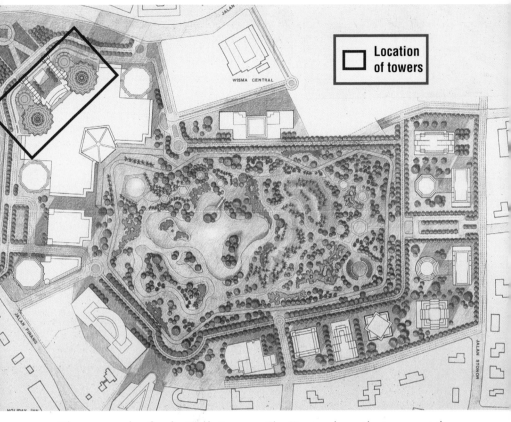

The master plan for the Kuala Lumpur City Center places the towers at the entrance of a complex that includes a park, shops, and hotels.

case towers. The winning design was by Cesar Pelli & Associates of the United States.

Pelli, the former dean of Yale University's School of Architecture, is an expert at designing tall buildings. He is known for his tall buildings throughout the United States and around the world. His Canary Wharf Tower in London, England, at 777 feet, is the tallest building in Great Britain.

In designing the Petronas Twin Towers, Pelli was charged with three main tasks. The owners wanted the buildings to be very tall. They wanted the buildings to form a gateway to the new city center. They also wanted the buildings to be modern yet reflect traditional Malaysian culture.

Sunlight reflects off the towers. To enhance the impression that the towers soar into the sky, Pelli designed the pinnacles to reflect light upward.

Towers That Soar

Pelli gave the owners impressively tall buildings by designing the towers to soar into the heavens. Every aspect of his design is geared toward projecting the towers upward. Pelli began by making the towers very slender. Their height is almost ten times their diameter. Pelli tapered the towers to make them seem even taller than they are. The tall, slender pinnacles also taper, as if to pierce the clouds. To make the pinnacles soar even more, the stainless steel is specially brushed so that light hitting it reflects upward.

Designing tall buildings is not easy. "The design of tall buildings is very demanding,"[3] Pelli writes. All of the practical requirements of a building, such as how it will be supported, become greater the taller the building.

One key to designing very tall buildings is to make sure they will be strong and stable. This is especially important when the buildings are the tallest in the world. Each tower empty weighs 330,690 tons, or about as much as sixty-six thousand elephants. The framework had to be strong enough to support this load plus the weight of all the people and furniture inside. Because floors are stacked in a tall building, doubling its height more than triples its load. Columns at the bottom of a tall building must be strong enough to support the weight of all of the floors above.

To support this tremendous weight, the engineers designed a framework of **high-strength concrete**. Most of the tallest skyscrapers, such as the Sears Tower, have steel frames or a combination of steel and concrete. Steel works well to frame tall buildings because it is extremely strong

The strong concrete framework of the towers supports the weight of the buildings and the furniture and people inside.

and lightweight. As engineers have found ways to make concrete stronger and less bulky, it is being used more often to frame tall buildings.

For the Petronas Twin Towers, the engineers designed a tube-in-tube framework. The inner tube is a gigantic, seventy-five-foot-square concrete **core** that forms a stiff spine at the center of each tower. The outer tube consists of sixteen super **columns** widely spaced around the edge of the building. They measure nearly eight feet across at the bottom and taper to about four feet across at the top. Concrete **beams** connect the columns to one another and to the central core.

Gateway in the Sky
The owners wanted the soaring towers to create a grand gateway to the new city center. To create this gateway the

architects highlighted the space between the towers. They did this in two ways. First, they made the towers identical and **symmetrical**. This arrangement gave the space between the towers a distinct shape of its own.

Second, the designers emphasized the space between the towers still more by adding a spectacular steel and glass skybridge. This bridge links the towers at the 41st and 42nd floors, 558 feet in the air. Pelli describes this magnificent gateway as "a 40-story-high portal to the sky."[4]

The steel and glass skybridge links the space between the towers. The skybridge and the towers form a gateway to the new city center.

Modern but Malaysian

Most importantly the owners wanted the towers to reflect Malaysia's culture while still being modern building. Incorporating Malaysian culture into the design was perhaps the most difficult task of all. Members of Pelli's team traveled throughout the country to experience firsthand Malaysia's culture and its people. Because Malaysia was a British colony until 1957, the young nation had little architecture of its own. Nor could Pelli look to the many high-rise buildings already in Kuala Lumpur. Most of them were built in the boxy style of the West. So he had to look elsewhere for inspiration. He found it in the geometric shapes that are common in the art of Islam, the country's national religion. Pelli explains what these shapes mean to Malaysians. "These geometric traditions are much more important in Islamic countries than in the West, and are understood, perceived, and appreciated by everyone in their society,"[5] he says.

Pelli chose an eight-pointed star for the shape of each building. The eight-pointed star is made by rotating a square on top of another square. In Islam, the eight-pointed star is a symbol of unity, harmony, stability, and rationality. To add more floor space to the design Pelli put half circles between the points of the star. The resulting shape has sixteen alternating points and curves, giving the outline of the towers a scallop border.

Stainless steel was chosen for the outside walls. Steel gives the towers a high-tech, modern look. It also shows its luster in Malaysia's tropical sun. The stainless steel re-

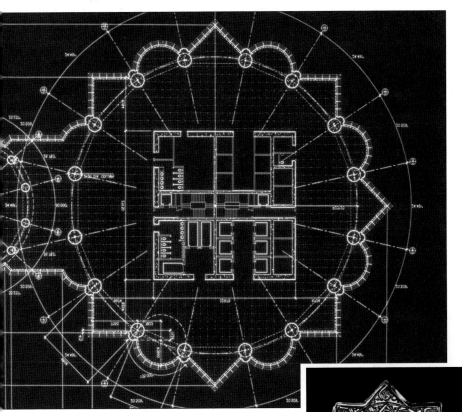

Pelli based his design for the towers
on the eight-pointed star (inset), a
symbol of stability in Islam.

flects the changing light of a
Malaysian day, changing in color
from gray to blue to yellow.

To alternate with the stainless steel, the designers
chose clear safety glass. The glass keeps out sound and
will not shatter. It has a special coating to help keep out
the heat and dangerous rays of the tropical sun. There are
thirty-three thousand windows in all, enough glass to
cover five city blocks. It takes window washers a month
to clean the windows in each tower. In this hot, tropical

21

Steel sunscreens and safety glass with a special coating protect people in the towers from the intense rays of the tropical sun.

country, shade is very important. So special sunscreens of steel piping were designed to hang over the windows.

After eight months of planning, construction was ready to begin on twin skyscrapers unlike any in the world. The design team had paid close attention to every detail to make sure construction would go smoothly. But many challenges—and some surprises—lay ahead.

From the Ground Up

Designing the super-tall towers was a major challenge, but construction would bring more hurdles. Never before had such a tall building been constructed in Malaysia. The country's tallest building at that time, Kuala Lumpur's Maybank Headquarters, measured only 799 feet. Building not one but two towers almost twice that height would require expertise, creativity, determination, and hard work.

In early 1993 the first challenge that construction workers faced was building strong **foundations** deep under the ground for the towers to rest on. Before work began a major problem arose. The original plan for the foundations called for massive **piers** that went down to solid rock called **bedrock**. Bedrock is the best material for supporting tall, heavy buildings. But late soil tests showed that the bedrock below the proposed towers formed a

The foundations of the Petronas Twin Towers are among the deepest in the world.

steeply sloping cliff. Building a foundation on a sloping cliff would be very expensive and could cause the towers to tilt. An engineer on the project explains the problem this way. "Building something there would be like beaching a boat," he says. "The bow is firmly on shore, while the stern floats on water."[6] The engineers solved this problem by moving the towers two hundred feet. In the new location, the buildings could rest entirely on soil, and a more uniform foundation could be built.

Super-Deep Foundation

The new location called for a completely different type of foundation—one of the deepest in the world. In the new design the foundation was comprised of many narrow supports, called **piles**, topped by a thick concrete mat. The mat spreads the weight of the towers to the piles, which gradually transfer it to the soil.

Construction workers first dug a deep hole for the towers' basements. Dirt from the hole filled five hundred trucks a day. Then workers bored 208 holes into the soil in order to build the piles. First a cage of steel bars was lowered into each deep, vertical hole. Then the hole was filled with concrete. The largest piles were about 9 feet by 4 feet in area and went down 377 feet, or about thirty stories underground. The piles work in the soil like huge nails.

Workers poured two fifteen-foot-thick concrete mats on top of the piles, one for each tower to rest on. To build each mat a steady stream of trucks dumped loads of concrete nonstop for two days. The concrete pours were the largest ever in Malaysia. The towers' foundations cost $52 million and took a year to build.

Trucks sit ready to dump concrete into the foundation. A steady line of trucks poured concrete into the foundation nonstop for two days.

Twins Rising Together

Once the foundations were laid, workers started on the massive concrete framework to hold up the twin towers. Both towers went up at the same time, with a separate crew working on each building. Each morning a team met to map out the details of that day's work. Crews worked around the clock seven days a week under the hot sun and pouring rain. More than two thousand people from several different countries worked on the towers.

Workers built the core walls first by pouring high-strength concrete into huge steel containers called forms. Once the concrete had set the forms were removed and

Huge containers of steel held concrete in place until it hardened.

Separate crews worked around the clock on both towers at the same time.

then moved to the next level. Next workers built the sixteen concrete columns and the ring beams tying them together. For the floors workers installed steel beams and decking and then poured on a thin layer of concrete. Using mostly steel for the floors eliminated many of the steps required in building all-concrete floors, making the work go faster. Crews worked on at least four levels of the towers at any one time. Most floors took four days to complete. To make sure that enough high-quality concrete was always available, a concrete plant was built right on the site.

A main concern in building the tall, slender towers was keeping them completely straight as they rose. If any level tilted, the double-deck elevators would not work. Nor would the towers be stable and strong. So every twelve hours experts used special measuring instruments to check that the towers were straight from top to bottom. To make the testing as accurate as possible, the same person used the same instrument at the same time each day.

Lifting the Skybridge

Probably the most dramatic feat of all was the lifting of the two-level, 794-ton skybridge into place. The 192-foot-long walkway was built and tested in South Korea before being taken apart and shipped to Malaysia in 493 pieces. The lifting crew was prepared. For more than a year they tested the lifting operation under various wind and weather conditions.

Before the lift began workers assembled the pieces on the ground into their main parts: two pairs of leg supports, two ends, and the center section. Then, using jacks, workers lifted the leg supports and attached them to the towers. Next the end sections went up and were attached temporarily to make sure the center section could fit between them.

Finally the big moment arrived. The large, heavy center section was ready to be raised to a height of 558 feet.

Under clear, sunny skies the prime minister pushed a lever to start the lift. The center section crept upward slowly to ensure that it would not be dropped. All went well until evening, and then a storm struck. Lightning knocked out the controls, stopping the lift in midair. Repairs were made and the lift resumed. But lightning struck again. Finally, after three anxious days, the center section was in place. Later the end blocks were permanently connected, and the tops of the leg supports were secured under the bridge. The "portal to the sky" was ready to welcome all.

Attached to very strong cables and lifting jacks, the center section of the skyridge is ready to be hoisted to its final position high above the ground.

Construction teams hoist the unfinished pinnacles into place from inside the towers.

Raising the Pinnacles

The raising of the 194-ton steel pinnacles in mid-February of 1996 was the crowning achievement. Each pinnacle was about as tall as a twenty-story building. Once the 241-foot-tall pinnacles were in place, the towers would be the tallest buildings in the world.

Construction teams hoisted the pinnacles from inside the towers. Because each pinnacle consists of many pieces, this, too, was a painstaking process. The pinnacles had to be assembled and lifted into place.

By mid-March of 1996 both pinnacles were in place. The skyline of Kuala Lumpur had been dramatically changed forever. And Malaysia and the world had two new tallest buildings.

Stiff, Strong, and Safe

The slender Petronas Twin Towers soar more than a quarter of a mile into the sky. For such tall, slender buildings wind is a major concern. While all tall buildings move in the wind, slender ones tend to sway even more. Some sway is necessary just as it is for tall trees. But buildings cannot sway too much or people inside will feel like they are getting seasick. Engineers have found that tall buildings can sway about three feet in any direction. As long as the movement is slow, it will not bother people inside.

Resisting the Wind

Kuala Lumpur has a favorable climate for tall buildings. The city is not subject to earthquakes, nor are high winds generally a problem. Kuala Lumpur is sheltered from the main force of monsoon winds because of its location inland from the South China Sea. However occasionally, about once every fifty years, wind gusts of sixty-five miles per hour hit the city. So engineers had to design the towers to withstand these rare gusts. To test the buildings' strength in high winds, the engineers used a **wind tunnel**. A wind tunnel allows engineers to test how air affects buildings, aircraft, and other objects. The engineers tested the towers using both actual and computer models.

The towers passed the wind tests with high marks, largely because of their concrete frames. Whereas steel

Engineers use wind tunnels like this one to test how strong winds affect buildings, aircraft, and other objects.

tends to be flexible, a concrete frame makes a building very stiff, so it can resist the force of the wind. The mass of the concrete also damps, or slows down, movements caused by the wind. Had steel frames been used for the towers, engineers would have had to add a device to cut down on sway.

Several other design elements of the towers reduce the effects of wind. The tapering of the towers exposes less area near the top where winds tend to be faster. The round shape of the towers is also affected less by wind than a rectangle would be. Because of their design the

Engineers use a model of the twin towers to study the buildings' design elements.

Cesar Pelli carefully checks a drawing of the towers to ensure that everything is just right.

towers' movement is very slow. Office workers feel comfortable even though the tops of the towers move back and forth slightly every nine seconds.

The Moving Skybridge

With the towers constantly moving, how does the skybridge between them stay attached? Solving that problem was a major engineering feat. Never before had engineers built a sky-high walkway between two super-tall towers. The engineers solved the problem by making the bridge connections flexible. The ends of the bridge slide in and out of the towers about a foot as the buildings move. When the towers move in the same direction, the bridge follows. When the towers move in opposite directions, the bridge stays put. The leg supports that keep the bridge centered also are flexible. Each leg ends at a **ball joint**, which works like a hip joint, to allow movement.

Fire Safety

A major danger in a tall building is fire. Fire-truck ladders can reach only the lower floors of a tall building. High-rise building fires have occurred beyond the reach of ladders. A 1988 fire at Los Angeles First Interstate Bank (in California) burned out the 12th to 16th floors. A 1991 fire at Philadelphia's One Meridian Plaza (in Pennsylvania) blazed from the 22nd to the 30th floors. Firefighters had to fight these fires from inside the building. In Kuala Lumpur, heavy traffic is another problem for firefighters. Designers of the Petronas Twin Towers experienced the city's crowded streets firsthand and knew fire trucks might have trouble reaching a fire quickly.

To overcome these problems the towers have modern technology for fighting a fire internally. Like most newer skyscrapers the buildings have water sprinklers designed to put out most fires before they spread very far. To make the sprinklers more reliable, each tower has a basement water-storage tank automatically filled from a city water main.

The devastating One Meridian Plaza fire illustrated the importance of sprinklers. Fire broke out on a Saturday evening on the high-rise building's twenty-second floor. Firefighters battled the blaze unsuccessfully for

Three firefighters lost their lives when this skyscraper in Philadelphia caught fire. A firefighter on a ladder can only effectively fight fires in smaller buildings (inset).

many hours. Only when the fire reached the thirtieth floor, which had sprinklers, was the blaze finally put out. None of the other burned floors had sprinklers.

In the Petronas Twin Towers if fire breaks out on a floor, it is automatically isolated by pressurizing the floors above and below it. This keeps smoke from traveling through the building. The smoky air can be removed from the building, and occupants can be safely evacuated to smoke-free floors.

This drawing of the towers shows the escape routes people can use in case of fire or other emergency.

The towers also have a Central Fire Command Center, staffed around the clock. The center is linked to smoke and heat detectors, sprinkler system monitors, and a public address system. Firefighters can speak to each other and to command-center staff using a two-way intercom found in all parts of the buildings.

Escape Routes

Like all high-rise buildings the towers have several escape routes. One is the skybridge. Lobbies at both ends of the bridge are fire refuge areas with their own air supply. If fire breaks out in one tower, occupants can walk across the skybridge to the other tower and take the elevators to safety. The towers have seventy-six elevators, most of them high-speed double-deckers, which can carry fifty-two people. Two elevators are only for use by firefighters.

Two stair exits lead from the upper floors of the towers and three from the lower floors. The stairs can be pressurized to keep out fire and smoke. In addition the stairs and elevators are inside the massive concrete core. With walls up to 2.5 feet thick, the core can keep out fire and smoke and is unlikely to be damaged. Tower occupants can reach a safe stairway within thirty-six minutes. Either building can be completely emptied in eighty minutes.

The towers also have several backup safety features. These include two kinds of backup lighting for the stairs, and backup pumps and hoses should the sprinklers fail. Several generators can provide backup electricity, a safety feature proved important by the First Interstate Bank fire. In that blaze an electrical failure shut down fans keeping

The Petronas Twin Towers dominate Kuala Lumpur's skyline. They will symbolize Malaysia's pride far into the future.

smoke out of the building's stairways, forcing several people to be rescued from the roof by helicopter.

The Petronas Twin Towers are built to pierce the sky above Kuala Lumpur far into the future. While most areas of the towers are off-limits to the general public, visitors are allowed on the skybridge every day but Monday. Standing high on this gateway in the sky, one can experience close up the towering beauty and majesty of the two tallest buildings in the world. Malaysians know that taller buildings will rise to take the world height record. Some are already in progress. But the Petronas Twin Towers are much more than a record. These beautiful, unique buildings will forever soar as a symbol to the world of a proud Malaysia.

Notes

Chapter 1: A Soaring Symbol

1. Quoted in Rashid Yusof, "PM Opens World's Tallest Building in Glittering Ceremony," *New Straits Times-Management Times*, September 1, 1999.

2. Cesar Pelli and Michael J. Crosbie, *Petronas Towers*. Chichester, UK: Wiley-Academy, 2001, p. 8.

Chapter 2: Designing Towers to Reach the Sky

3. Pelli, *Petronas Towers*, p. 8.

4. Pelli, *Petronas Towers*, p. 9.

5. Quoted in Denise Laitinen, "Touching the Stars: Malaysia's Petronas Towers," *National Fire Protection Association (NFPA) Journal*, May/June 2001, p. 67.

Chapter 3: From the Ground Up

6. Udom Hungspruke, quoted in Mark Wheeler, "The World's Tallest Building," *Popular Mechanics*, May 1996, p. 78.

Glossary

ball joint: A joint in which a ball moves within a holder called a socket.

beams: Horizontal supports for a structure.

bedrock: The solid rock layer below the soil.

columns: Vertical supports for a structure.

core: Central region of a skyscraper.

foundations: The strong base built under the ground that supports a structure.

high-strength concrete: Concrete with special materials added to make it extra strong. Basic concrete consists of water, sand, small stones, and a gray powder called cement.

master plan: A plan giving overall guidance.

minarets: Tall, slender towers of a mosque, from which a person calls worshipers to prayer.

mosque: A Muslim place of worship.

piers: Vertical structural supports.

piles: Vertical columns driven or built underground to support a structure.

pinnacles: The upper tapering parts of a building.

symmetrical: Having a balanced grouping of parts on either side of a line.

wind tunnel: A chamber for testing the effects of wind on buildings, aircraft, and other objects.

For Further Exploration

Books

Carol A. Johmann, *Skyscrapers! Super Structures to Design & Build*. Charlotte, VT: Williamson, 2001. Lets the reader be an architect or engineer of a skyscraper through many hands-on activities, including building a model of the Petronas Twin Towers.

Elaine Landau, *Skyscrapers*. New York: Childrens Press, 2001. Describes the history and building of skyscrapers and features some of the world's tallest.

Cesar Pelli and Michael J. Crosbie, *Petronas Towers*. Chichester, UK: Wiley-Academy, 2001. This book by the architect of the towers is not written for children, but young people will be fascinated by the many pages of sketches, drawings, models, and photos of the Petronas Twin Towers at every stage.

Video

David Macaulay, "Building Big: Skyscrapers," South Burlington, VT: WGBH Boston Video, 2000. Provides a close-up look at tall buildings throughout history, including the Petronas Twin Towers.

Websites

Building Big: All About Skyscrapers (www.pbs.org). Explains skyscraper basics and features several well-known skyscrapers, including the Petronas Twin Towers. Includes a lab section on how tall buildings resist the wind and other forces.

KLCC Group of Companies: Project Showcase: Petronas Twin Towers (www.klcc.com.my). This official website of the Kuala Lumpur City Center has a wealth of information, photos, and diagrams of the Petronas Twin Towers.

Skyscrapers.com (www.skyscrapers.com). This site provides information and photos on the Petronas Twin Towers and thousands of other skyscrapers around the world. It also has a list of the two hundred tallest.

Index

Picture Credits

About the Author

Author Janet Halfmann has written many nonfiction books for children and young adults. Her books include several on architecture—on the subjects of mosques, theaters, and Greek temples. This is her second book for Kid-Haven Press. She previously wrote about scorpions in the Nature's Predators series. Halfmann is a former children's activity book writer and editor, children's magazine editor, and daily newspaper reporter. When she is not writing, Halfmann works in her garden, explores nature, and spends time with her family.